# Still Life with Poppies: Elegies

# Still Life with Poppies: Elegies

Poems by

Leslie Schultz

Kelsay Books

Cover art: Lanesboro, Minnesota (Leslie Schultz, 2015)
Poet's photograph: Sally Nacker

ISBN 13:978-0692627426

*Kelsay Books*
Aldrich Press
www.kelsaybooks.com

*This book is for Timothy Braulick, who helps to carry
every sorrow and who magnifies every joy*

# Acknowledgments

Grateful acknowledgment is made to the editors of the publications in which the following poems originally appeared (some in slightly different form).

*A Nuclear Vision:* (Video by Art Positive and Survival Graphics for Hiroshima Day) "A Dream of Sacrifice"

*Mezzo Cammin*: "On Biography"

*Poetic Strokes Anthology:* "The Book of Quilts"

*Swamp Lily Review:* "Memento Mori" and "Orpheus"

*The Northern Review:* "Duluth"

*The Pacific Review:* "For Kurt: Who's Missing"

*The Wayfarer:* "Black Swans"

*Winona Media:* "Triptych," "Sudden Departure," and "A Candle for Maggie Lee"

"Jazz" is published by the City of Northfield, Minnesota—stamped into the concrete of sidewalks as part of the Sidewalk Public Poetry Project.

"Premonition", in slightly different form, originally appeared in a chapbook, *Living Room* (Leslie Schultz Black, Midwestern Writers' Publishing House)

"Sleeping Beauty in Potter's Field" first appeared in *Everything Comes to Light* (Leo Luke Marcello, editor, The Cramer's Press)

*Some friends are essential not only to life but to art. I give my abundant thanks to these especially, my circle of readers, cheerleaders, and well-wishers, without whom I could not have written these poems or collected them into a book.*

To Sally Nacker, friend of the heart and the work for many years, who was there as these poems were born and who always knew there would be a book.

To Stella Nesanovich, whose keen eye and generous heart helped burnish the manuscript in the homestretch, and to:

Julia Braulick
Timothy Braulick
Beth Clary
Julia Denne
Bonnie Jean Flom
Ellen Keller
Ann Lacy
Marilyn Larson
Jan Newman
Karla Schultz
Julia Uleberg Swanson
Carolyn Warden

*You each have my heartfelt thanks.*

# Contents

Notes
About the Author

# I. That Essential Font

# On Biography

*to those I leave behind*

I would write a book that cannot burn,
a book of clear-running water,
complete, with song and wisdom—stern
as my beautiful daughter.

All biography ends in death.
All lifelines run their seaward course.
Read me again, while you have breath,
until you know my secret's source.

# A Dream of Sacrifice

I begin to sink,
a light ballet in the dim, green air.

My hair floats and weaves around my arms like sea grass.

I sink the slow, polished arabesque a statue makes
thrown to appease the sea,

but the sea collapses,
grows primitive and still
like the heart of an emerald, inhuman.

I reach the chill water, and see you,
and continue to sink, colder with each meter.

Our skins luminesce.

I see stone walls,
fear in your eyes,
bones on the bottom, weighted with gold.

Ooze closes on my toes
until I push muscles, breath, blood

at dead water and begin
to sunlight an uncertain ascent.

# Encountering Catacombs

Parisian streets hold many wonders.
Consider those stacked walls of books
piled like intricate building stones
behind the clear antiquarian door
of Shakespeare and Company—just one
of a thousand caves of delight.

One door, back then, led to a spiral stair.
I descended, carrying a candle.
By its pale essential light
I read, as I walked those halls
built of bodies rent asunder,
that essential font of dry bones.

I walked those woeful corridors,
protecting my brief candle;
young, afraid. Not cursing the darkness
but filling with slant echoes:
a reader newly alive
to the power of scripts to sunder.

There, in that dolorous crypt,
that library of earth-bleached bones,
I became a living pebble, thrown
into the common pool of words
finding by slow accretion—
echolocation—
my own heartbeat, my own poems.

# My Father Confessor

*for my teacher, Leo Luke Marcello*

You almost wore a black robe, and so
you understood how to craft
the life of an American saint
in poems glowing like haloed

Apollo. Remember Galleria Luca?
Your brother's transcendent oils
leaning against the wainscoting,
near your bayous, waiting? One, cubic, a

symphony of crossed golds and blues
called "Flight Out of Egypt"—
Chris's memory of travel,
then your poem, then his canvas:

these nest together now
on my wall near the source
of the Mississippi. Leo,
recall we saw a mandala born, how

the gentle Tibetan monks
blew colored sand into a circle,
a map of heaven? They defied tradition,
did not send it down the river's steep banks

into eternity. Just this one rests
at the Minneapolis Institute of Art,
caught in a net of polymers
by pre-arrangement with scientists

from 3M. You were visiting
and later a poem called you,
all those streaming hues
were joy and elegy mingling.

Leo, I confess no sin, just what
you must know: I miss you so;
the way you bit into life
as if into an olive, black and tart;

the laser of your light-and-dark mind;
how you held the made
and the growing worlds
in your heart. You made a wrenched,

black absence when you left
that weaves into my art.

# Homesick

*for Dorothy and William Wordsworth*

Lonely bones, an old house, long abandoned,
just beyond the curve of that rushing stream.

No one now can know the life it nourished:
its hearth stone cold, scoured clean even of ash;
its cupboards bare; its sink dry as grave dust.

As tombs are little houses for the dead,
this suite of rooms once alive, the machine
and carapace of loving family life,
stands, silent, in its copse of fragrant trees,
memorial to what once moved within:
breath of sleeping children, flickering light,
deep chill seeping past ice-ferned window panes.

And now grey dust reigns down a gentle night.
Do you hear? Keening beneath autumn rains?

# Model of a Watchtower

China, Han Dynasty, 1st century C.E.; Minneapolis Institute
  of Art

*for my friend, who carries beads of memory on the last march*

Empty windows, dark as departed souls:
three rectangles crowned by one coal-black square.
Six figures squat and wait: four below,
bellicose; the two aloft serenely seeing far

off, across the contested plain, watching slow
undulations of the river's currents,
larks that soar and dip, swifts and swallows,
the tumbling seasons, all wild life's torrents.

These high sages balance near towering clouds
knowing this fragile tower—baked red clay
girt by a green-glazed wall—is made of clods;
each key-shaped moon gate pointing toward decay.

Someday, the watch fires will be lit. The cock
cresting the roof will crow with shrill alarms;
night will smash down like a fiery black rock;
And life's brief smoke will drift—past present harms.

What do we living watch for, with every breath?
Armies of oblivion? Advancing death?

# Mortua Est

*for Shirley Marie Pressel Warden*
*October 5, 1935 - June 2, 2015*

I cannot quite believe it, but it is true.
Among the ancient green hills of Cincinnati—
are there seven?—she is lying still,
like a white stone on the shore
of the shining Ohio. A fallen star.

I can still hear her laughter,
her singing voice. See her tending
to whatever was needed: bending
over the garden pool with a net
to clear the surface of fallen leaves
so others could splash and play;
coaching illiterate children in their letters;
guiding families through protean wonders
at the vast Cincinnati zoo.

Rare as the shy okapi she loved,
beautiful as the Shirley poppy that shares her name,
my aunt, nearly eighty, is now high above
the flow of time, the fields of pain
where we, unmoored by her vanished wake,
drift, uncertain, in the awful calm.

# Still Life with Poppies

*Lanesboro, Minnesota*


Mist in the valley at dawn
sifts over thin clusters of poppies
rising—yellowy-orange, stems of thin green—

from between that mythical rock
and a hard place. garden wall and side walk.
Life seeks that fine line we must all walk,

finds a fertile edge between
twin implacable mysteries—
striving to bloom, scattering seed.

Here is where I plant hesitant filaments—
seedlings of vision and ritual—
one candle, one brief dance of flame.

# The Scattering

*August 18, 2015—for Aunt Shirley*

In the morning,
early, still ur-dark,
when I tip a little cream
into the liquid shadows
of my morning tea,
sudden white clouds
swirl like the cosmos
for half a breath
before diffusing completely,
dyeing the whole brew
the same pale hue.

So, too, your ashes danced
on the breeze over the cold,
sun-sparkled waters
of Lake Superior last
Tuesday when we released them
from a tight-stoppered bottle
of clear glass—sending them
with poems and prayers and music;
a flotilla of found, white feathers;
fragments of dried monarch wings;
fallen maple leaves streaked
red and green—into the vastness
of this inland ocean.

First on the light breeze,
then on the sunlit surface,
then suspended, in motion,
over the mottled sand,
your shape briefly echoed
the starry clouds from which you

were born, Aunt Shirley,
in the vast cauldron of stars,
as we all are. It is fitting
that you—part of you—can rest
lightly here, under the powerful
currents of the vastest earthly sea
of freshest water, in the most beautiful place
I know: Little Sand Bay.

Such a humble name
for such a spot of power.
Birch, maple, fir,
wind, water, wave,
sun, stars, bonfires,
tumbled stones, beach glass,
mosquitoes and red fox,
brown bear and green grass,
speckled fawns, terns,
wild pea plants, dragon flies—
like them we are drawn here,
over and over.

As you soar down,
like genie smoke
toward your transformation
into mystery and story,
our hearts lift
slightly,
as we strive to let go
of you, succumb
to light.

# II. Russet and Flame

# Premonition

It is winter. While we are out walking
together, my brother and I startle
a wild grouse. It rises, russet and flame,
toward the setting sun, then it grows too bright
to follow. I insist it is a vision.

The fields are sharp with stubble, so we go
carefully, hoping to spring another,
hoping to be ready this time
to hear its angry clamor.
Instead our shadows grow long and black
and the fields remain shut:
but then I turn to my brother and see
the anger in him, the consuming flames.

# For Kurt, Who's Missing

Some of you rests, I know, in the red clay
decanter you glazed and fired at school,
its garland of green leaves now sealed
in an ill-lit memorial corridor, ranked
third from the bottom, third from the right,
near the stained-glass window immured from sun
but still triumphant, fluorescing,
the one depicting a haloed redeemer, our mother's idea.

The rest of you
we shook on the wind-scoured icy graves
of our father's kin.
Specks of you burned our eyes.

We'd agreed. We stood, family, circling the white bed
for the body's unbearable last shudders.
Later, the need for relics immense,
I witnessed the twisted husk of your pride, sky-blue,
a Dodge, in the locked police garage,
and pocketed shattered glass,
a broken knob from the dash.

# Rhymes Chanted for Kurt

When you were a small boy
we bandaged your head,
your sister and I,
your sister,
and put you to bed.

With strips of rotting sheet
we wrapped your legs and arms,
told you to keep
very still,
worked magic charms,

made you fake a limp.
You gave us our way,
swallowed our thin tea
of willow leaves
without asking pay

or running to Mother.
Determined to cure
your health,
we ran away,
thinking you lay secure

in splints and torn gauze.
But tired of playing lame,
you came after us,
making us mad:
we hated to lose the game

to truth.
Today you lie still—
an ash muting
a glare of snow,
crowning this winter hill,

while we stare, our eyes red
at what is undone, unsaid.

# Entry and Echo

| | |
|---|---|
| curt | Kurt |
| adj. | a brother,<br>a loss beyond description |
| orig. short or shortened | was it in the naming?<br>an unwished curse? |
| brief, to the point of rudeness | absence intrudes |
| terse or brusque | there is no adequate reply |
| SYN.  see blunt | the dulling edge<br>of unrelinquished pain,<br>the compelling drip<br>on jagged stone |

# March 3, 2015

This is what the light was like then,
on the cold morning you were born.
Nineteen sixty-three. That is when
you emerged from our mother's torn

body, the umbilical cord
wrapt tight around your throat three times,
your body blue, stiff as a board.
While machines sounded inhuman chimes,

she nearly died, and so did you.
That was pain for another day,
another March, with shadows blue
and long, the tattered snow shroud-grey.

Before daffodils bloom each year,
Kurt, my brother, I feel you here.

# Triptych

*for Jennifer Bonner*

## I. The River

Daily I listen for the Great Door Slam
to echo through the house of the body.
I know that a wild silence is coming,
without echoes to tell me what I am.

The dissolution of the blood and bone
does not come easily or slow enough,
(despite its long unfolding over years)
to catch the shape and color of our tears.

Tears fall abundantly from us all,
a slow-motion plummeting waterfall.
The water in the body seeks to join
a common cascade, like a silver shawl

flung on a chair, like a brook's quiet song.
The river that our dreams travel nightly along
towers finally over our heads, fills our ears,
and rages into silence, smashing fears.

When the wind has custody of the breath,
trembling sweetens into the roar of death.
All coalesces into one loud slam—
and the 'I' dissolves to discover the 'am'.

II. Halloween Costume

Above my desk this photograph of you is
hung in all your glory. Real gloria.
A strand of tiny electric lights winds about
your slim body, Jennifer. Your right hand,
like the nightly pulse of the lighthouse,
flashes light back at the camera lens while
your arms create your own, hard-won halo.

That October, while you contemplated your heart,
not knowing if it would last, you remembered to live
in the moment. And so for Halloween you became
One Thousand Points of Light, scoffing at a candidate's
rhetoric but also redeeming it, flinging
a constellation of courage against the growing dark.

III. Saying Grace

Just this:
despite your father's daily grief,
your mother's bent head,

your empty place at the table still
nourishes us all
like bread.

# Sudden Departure

*for Ana Ortiz de Montellano*

Yesterday, when I heard, the sky
over our shared fields was grey,
the trees bare or flaming or flying burnt-out banners,
acquiescing to this season of early frosts.

I carry two sharp memories of you
moving silently through the ripening crops,
placing each foot carefully, gazing down,
wrapped in a cloak of solitude; and

as a whirling blur of motion,
twin swords flashing,
painting the fierce Mother Form before us,
a precision of will and surrender, limb and breath.

Three memories, each keen. The last, in spring,
in sunshine, rocking on my porch, speaking your love
of words, your hand gentle on my daughter's head,
your smile warm and sweet. Three pictures,
far too few.

I mourn with one lit candle this grey dawn.
You are not forgotten, though too soon gone.

# Grave Goods

Little piece of burnt pottery,
glazed in the southwest
a thousand years ago,
made to keep water safe
in this vast dry land,
you, compass—now marooned
in a sea of hammered silver,
reined by a leather thong
around my own neck—

Teach me how to shape
my life, to surf over
dark waves of pain, to see the best
in myself when I'm quivery
on this earth. The moon's bow
shines on the dry wreck
of my needs. My song,
fainter, is evidently tuned
to the crystalline desert sand.

# III. Plumbago

# Winter Evenings, Lake Mendota

Every winter evening it's the same.
The lake lies bare against the blue night,
the bus flies
over the dam and locks.
I pull the bellcord, I think ahead
to the brick apartments, blocks
composed of blocks, to dark
evergreens in the courtyard, the lamp
in our window, and the icy walks,
the rigid geometry of the walks.
Days fold like cardboard boxes.
Every night I think, *Tonight I will not*
*stop. I will make myself small*
*on the back seat and sleep*
*until the sun breaks up the ice.*
But always there is the lamp
in our window, fire behind the locked door.

# Duluth

This is true north;
it is more fixed than heaven.
Beyond icy shallows
the deeps steam.
Anchors stay hidden.
Their chains seem to end
where they touch the lake,
yet these ships are linked to them
tenuously
as dreams nearly dreamed.
Hulls full of grain
float in a cold slumber.
I wonder why we've come,
whether we're late or early.
It's Sunday.
The sun hangs
on the quiet derricks,
sunk,
leaking daylight.
We huddle in the car,
holding black coffee
while our words dissolve.
Only the coast retains
an air of permanence.
We're lost.
A loon cries;
its shadow rises
like breath or smoke.

# Deep in Louisiana

Tonight if our ceiling
fan loosed its blades
would they wheel through the window
like dark birds, prehistoric,
moon-maddened? Or
would we dream ourselves
grass, heads heavy
and ready for the haying?

# The Burn Ward

*for Geoffrey McCleery Black*

Click. The door locks behind me and I know
I am in the wrong place. We are together;
there is no turning back.

The beds are draped in white, like tents
or shrouds, a darkness all too visible
and dazzling to our pain-dimmed eyes.

Behind us, upstairs and down a blood-flecked
hall, your mother no longer knows what is wrong,
why we keep screaming for her nurses.

I have held her as she strained not to soil
anything, shook to keep her balance. You helped her
the way you knew, insisting on needles and white pills.

Now she is sleeping fitfully, her arms twitching
with nightmare, while we slip away for coffee.
But where are we? In a cavern of silent agony.

A landscape of scorch, of sticky ointment and blisters
like raging seas. We do not speak or touch, fearing
our own infection. I step forward, instinctively, trying

not to look. And I think I hear you following. No
Orpheus, I am not even tempted
to turn, certain you are still with me, still of this earth.

# The Boatman Praises Sleep

*Lake Charles, Louisiana*
  *for Geoffrey McCleery Black*


From the pier, shrimp boats drift away, as though
they drag the dawn in their nets – the new day,
that golden bugle, doomed but not yet
tarnished. Later, bow by bow, the boats will bump
the moorings, the motors will die, the crying gulls
will wheel overheard excited by the stink
of gasoline and shell fish lifted to light.

Since March, I've had trouble sleeping.
So I endure the pressure of an airless night
as best I can, then walk to the lake with
coffee, searching for a little breeze.
My recent troubles compound themselves daily,
grow intricate, Florentine, Byzantine.
My wife has left me. I see no way out,
my head a black hole where all the colors
drain away, slip through the net of day, catch
vast, cold currents, are ferried to sleep at last.

# To a Silent Orderly

Hospitals are fearsome places, devoid
of rest, stewing with contagions, brisk with
techniques, theoretical and applied,
designed to chivvy health from grey unhealth.

Are hospitals as fearsome as my body?
With all its working parts and processes—
wet, microbial—an electric sea
humming like a vast, unknowable city?

I imagine, from the penthouse of my brain,
I oversee—as mayor—streets, repairs,
garbage collection, sewers, that looming crane,
removal chutes, and poised jackhammers.

Conductor, in your white and blood-flecked coat—
my train of thought departs for Charon's boat.

# A Marriage

On the banks of the Sugar River
they peddled their chromium mile.
They would glance at each other and smile,
then look away and shiver.

The man with the burning beard
and the lady with too-large eyes
entered a country they feared
despite its radiant skies.

Around them the scenery flew—
the rushes, the milkweed and tar,
the cinders blown in from afar.
The hot sky hung heavy and blue.

The man and the lady grew breathless,
pumping for all they were worth,
imagining love could be deathless.
Now the man burns under the earth.

# Interlude

Lady Macbeth, laving her hands,
stood by the open door.
She gazed without seeing the falling leaves.
Her heart was shriveled and sore.

Her fingers the color of heavy cream
and her knuckles like luminous stones
grew shiny and red, like nettle fire,
as she kneaded the flesh from its bones.

She worked to wear away the flesh
like the sea caresses the sand,
imperceptibly smoothing away
the beach from the rocky strand.

Wind rattled and jarred her ancient eaves
with the promise of early snow.
It carried with it, close to its heart,
a sense of vertigo

brought by swirls of drying husks,
a haunting in amber and gold.
Undone, she kept her face a mask,
raised to the stinging cold.

# When You Visit Pluto's Realm

I.

You must go alone. It will be
crowded on the ferry dock
but the one-way ticket
you didn't reserve
waits in your name only.
You must pay for it
with all you have left—
two silver coins, one vast sigh.
It is not possible
to cancel
when your name is called.
A chill wind blows. The gangplank
creaks. You smell oily waters.
In the burnt-out coal of your heart
there remains one ember
of desire:
to cross the burning river,
to reach the land of fire.

II.

The sickening music of the oars beats down,
over and over, on the water, lifting the stench.
This garbage scow slides at cross-purposes
to Styx. Here the sewaged flow of time
tugs against the pulse of eternity.

Even this nightmare journey lasts forever.

You, hollow-eyed, dry-tongued, lean on the railing,
aching, as the last fevers of longing
for your past life lift like vapors
from your cooling mind, your torso.
The boatman steers not by stars
but by stony echolocation,
an essential churning. Oars, poles,
ropes, stinking gasoline engines,
endless chanting dirges—all pull
this barge toward your destination,
Abyss, the City of Dis-
interest, where you will dully
disembark. Yet, when the prow thuds
against the oozing shore (the craft secure,
the gangplank in place) and you—visitor
or immigrant—lurch forward, you note
a remnant under your tongue, a thin disk
of shining silver, token of who you were,
something still lingering, a thing capable
of conjuring the sullen but sunlit world.

III.

Expanding, the silver coin spins into a sphere—
like a shining bubble of soap—

and your memories reappear,
shimmer, as if in a globe of glass:

hope, all the flowering meadows,
lonely flutes, warm hearts you've known,

and all flecked with passions of sweet
and violent hue, the crushed perfume

50

of song and desire,
everything you've made and failed to make.

This spinning globe invites you
to reawaken.

IV.

It dawns on you that choice lingers,
a return ticket fraying in your pocket,
although you have been naked a long time.

It makes no sense, but you see
one single prick of light:
for a moment more, before

you step onto the shore
of the Land of Unmaking
forever, you have the power

to rise past the stone sky, pass
through the tangled roots,
re-enter the Country of Making,

and, if you do, you must carry seeds
from the City of Dis—disease,
disenchantment, disrepair.

Ever after, you will be called to deploy
your ransomed part of a singer's dark
and incandescent art.

# Plumbago

*for Geoffrey McCleery Black*

You were teetering on the brink
of suicide when I met you.

In Lake Charles, you planted young trees,
crepe myrtles, outside the kitchen

window of our old rented house.
You knew how to do that: dig down

through turf, loosen reluctant roots,
offer mulch and water. You knew

so much more than I did about
so much: music, literature,

those lush sub-tropical landscapes
of Louisiana, leaden

solder of infamous shipyards,
and rain. Rain every day, rusting

the bewildered blue plumbago
and the rivets of your cracked heart.

# IV. Eclipse at Solstice

# The House on East Broad Street

Did they think it would always be there for them
when they sang around the piano at night
and joked about those new high-rise hems?

The house is still standing here, right
where it's always been, on the east bank
of the Fox River, within easy sight

of the Menasha Dam. As a boy, Grandpa once sank
his skiff, and would have gone over that wall
but he clung to a rail until they pulled him, rank

and boasting, from a frothy squall
of brown water. He had always been a strong
swimmer. Once he chased my beachball,

when the wind carried it like a song
in front of him, to the farthest end
of Five Mile Lake. "A foolish long

way to chase nineteen cents," Grandma said. "He'll spend
his strength." But he didn't. Today, I've
found where the family boathouse stood, at the little bend

where the current slows and ducks dive
through brackish water. Standing here on broken rocks,
in back of a house that was once alive

with songs, I squint to see where the old docks
joined the shore and try to hear
the swish of long skirts, the nightly winding of clocks.

Upstairs, the hardwood floors tilt toward the rear
of the house, toward the river. The small
servant's stairway has steps too high and sheer

for any but a child to navigate, and all
the taps spill rusty water. It's easy to see
why no one will buy the house. Someone might fall

on the sagging porch and sue. Besides, Aunt Izzie
lived here for years with all her cats, and the smell
will stay until the house goes. I have the key

but I don't go in. Some cousins are going to sell
the furniture, now that Izzie's gone.
Everybody's gone, and there's no one left to tell
how the piano sounded out across the lawn.

# Green Grapes

*for Grandma Phyllis*

The sky is milky with unfallen snow.
Green grapes, still attached to a length of stem,
rest on the deep indigo of the glass plate.

January in Minnesota. The sun is bedded down. The sky
must be indigo somewhere behind the clouds. Only
the two brightest ladies, slender Diana the chaste,
who leans toward Venus, her dazzling cousin, only
these two brilliants pierce through the heavy clouds.

My young daughter, grey-eyed like Athena,
rambunctious as Artemis, with hair as fiery-gold
as that of Botticelli's Venus, is sleeping
the sleep of angels, the sleep
that opens the gate hung with roses,
arching over the flagstone path that leads
to the underground river.

I pluck a single grape, crush it between my teeth. Sweet!
I expected sour musk. My grandmother kept fresh fruit
in a bowl, even in the expensive season. Green grapes,
delicate globes,
hung over the edge,
and I was allowed to eat my fill.

At home, we had waxy apples or bananas with spots,
sometimes fruit cocktail from a can, heavy with pears, jeweled
with a few gooseberries, a few scraps of dyed cherry.

Grandma had fresh coffee cake and pot roast that fell off the bone,
bread in a special drawer, cold milk with the taste of cream,

57

and hot coffee percolating in a chrome pot,
with a cheery red light and black cord curly
as a piglet's tail. She rolled out pie dough
with big, strong arms and painted fingernails,
scalloped potatoes with hot butter. At Christmas,
she made heavy chocolate balls laden with rum.

For years, her fingers were stained with nicotine,
her eyes in the evenings were glassy with stiff Manhattans,
red with tears. She could be a dirty fighter,
hissing the meanest thing, lips dark scarlet,
hair armored with permanent wave. I know
now her anger left its mark on my father (and so on me). And yet,
tonight, what is vivid is the comfort of her laugh,
the beauty and order of her home,
the bravery behind her choice of beautiful clothes.

When I was eight years old and lived two thousand miles away,
she came to visit. She took me shopping,
bought me a blue glass bowl on a tall stem, fluted like a shell,
bought me a package of white stones to fill it,
and, at my insistence, some plastic fruit to place in it:
a banana,
two perfect apples, an orange, a pear,
and, best of all,
a fat cluster of green grapes
that popped on and off their plastic stems.

Long after she left, I would reach for those grapes,
squeezing them, tasting them, trying to will
the scent of coffee and lemon polish,
a glimpse of those gleaming jars in her fruit cellar,
the sparkling panes of her diminutive French doors,

the sound of her ivory piano keys softly causing tiny
hammers to strike,
$$\text{strike,}$$
$$\text{strike}$$
like the sound of her high cream-colored heels at Easter, notes
perfect and disturbing as the glass eyes
set into the head of her mink stole, the one that bit its own tail
with the tiniest sharp teeth.

Tonight, Grandma, I think of how you wept
the last time I saw you, when I asked about your mother.
Then you told me of her cruelty.
I lift my glass to you,

a clear fluted goblet, gold leaf on the rim.
I drink the fiery ruby of grapes
crushed without their permission,
grapes that still hold onto their own power,
their unforgettable perfume.

# Egg Harbor, Wisconsin

The remaining grapes have dried,
their woody stems gone brittle,
their supporting lattice soft.
It's December. All week the winds
have increased, turning wet and brutal.
I walk through the arbor toward the sea wall
to find the fruit trees Father planted in spring.
Their young trunks, twisted, slick with rain,
do not block the view, or frame it.
They disturb, like permanent scratches
on a known photograph;
grey smoke, as I approach, before the uneasy bay,
darker when I circle behind them,
long smudges on the lighted house.
They won't survive this wind without cover.
Father can't now, so no one will tend them.

I think how it's been a hard fall, that perhaps
they're already dead, yet they stand
like reproach or hope.

# Eclipse at Solstice

*December 21-22, 2011*

I.

In December, an overlay of ash
touches everything, dims the sparkling
lights, dusts the holiday food. Even song
is numbed. This grief is the dust of the grave.

Gloom doesn't skew how I try to behave—
Cheery! Warm! I am a mother. It's wrong
to admit my spirit walks on darkling
plains, stumbling, careening for that sure crash,

vertiginous plunge from the balsam's peak
to under the shadowy feet of Claus,
Santa-Shiva, whose nose runs, whose eyes blear.
The nutcracker's wide, implacable jaws,
engine, manufacturing Christmas cheer,
have caught me up, as every year, this week.

II.

I know a woman who says that spring stands
for death in her personal lexicon.
She raises sheep. Ewes birth. Baby lambs die
not infrequently. Sometimes, ewes go mad

with grief for what they almost—almost—had.
Last night, the Full Moon in Cancer rode high,
eclipsed, then pierced the morning clouds laid on
our western hills like unwrapped swaddling bands.

Soon comes the morning when we open gifts.
There is so much I would give to the world
if I could, if I saw what to bestow.
This year, events have caught me, swept me, swirled
life and death into a new indigo.
I see how this vast night stains the snow drifts.

III.

Later, this knowledge will fade, but all true
sight lurks under other truths. Gentlemen
are not always merry or well at rest
when the old year leans into the shadows.

Do they wander Elysian meadows
or drift, smiling, near the Isles of the Blest
now that they have used their fine acumen
to still familiar flesh I loved and knew?

Twenty-four years ago, in flaming pride
and pain, my first husband courted Morpheus;
after the courts sundered us, man and wife,
and left me to weep: reluctant Orpheus.
Seven years ago, my father crushed his own life
using the hand on his right, tremored side.

IV.

This year I have painted a pair of skates,
shined the blades with silver glitter, tied them
up near the front door of our Victorian
house, studded a wreath with yellow roses,

arranged cut fir branches in green poses
of welcome, hiding the Hyperborian
chill my heart encloses deep down inside,
that smokes like dry ice on fine china plates.

Anger. Sorrows. Fears. Old corroding hate.
Not ornamental, surely, but stuck on
like burrs, like medals from forgotten wars
brought out for this annual occasion.
Brittle, they shatter on our polished floors:
these tinseled chains are not my ironclad fate.

V.

*for Bonnie Jean Flom*

There comes a loosening. A lightening.
A turn. Nothing so graceful as a leap
or a pirouette, but still....something small
moves, like a key, like tumblers in a lock,

something shiny, well-oiled, clean as a clock.
Tonight, a friend gave me silver charms, all
atremble with music and showing deep
knowledge of me, love, the need for brightening

laughter whenever our days are laced with pains.
So I breathe a little deeper for a space,
make jokes, taste something citrusy and cool,
begin to feel I can regain my place

of peace. Friendship is a heart-forged jewel.
My sorrows burst apart like paper chains.

# Home Place

On the cusp of middle age, I drive back
to Kalamazoo. I need to see what's true,
what might be addled by family story;
so I seek that rotted shell on Wall Street,
whose fragments of rooms I still remember,
the house my young parents purchased by chance.

Its entrance silted up now with roses,
its hardwoods softened by silver mushrooms,
this place I used to know in my cradle
looms stranger than a witch-ruined castle,
gloomier than any yew-shrouded manse,
more forlorn than a farmhouse gone to seed.

Not quaint. No hint of picturesque. Not quite.
There's a man face-down on the chipped front walk,
clutching a bottle, lost in fumes and dreams.
The striped awning is tattered, the shades down
nearly all the way, but I see a glimpse
of my start. I turn the key. I pull away.

# Crow Cries in April

When a crow screams at noon like an old rusty swing,
when violets erupt on lawns like a rash,
we're headed—again—for a colorized spring,
season of all that is raucous and brash.

When potholes appear like an unsightly pox,
when pollens ride in like witches on breezes,
when the ants come marching over the rocks
and into these houses beset with sneezes,

it's certainly spring, that sad time of year,
when hay fever paints our eyelids bright red;
each tulip is rabbit-munched down to its spear;
and lush weeds stand tall in the flower bed.

And—blast!—there goes Wordsworth bobbing along,
humming his bumbling daffodil song.

# When There is No Grave to Dance On

I dance like Wordsworth's daffodils—
shards of sunlight, shards of lake wave;
or make some iffy-jerky moves—
my thrilled version of the Moonwalk;
jog, maybe, panting (reciting
poems that pop into my glad brain),
over miles of sere woodland trails,
feeling glee as my chest heaves until

I stop.

When the blood pounding in
my ears clears and my breath slows down,
I wait by the river's edge, listen
to the geese and those raucous crows.
I watch the moon rise (luminous
maw), then raise my arms, lift my chin,
allow the old howl to begin—again.

# Revisiting the Marshland

*for Louise Glück, in response*


This place is musty—though still with the smell of char—
and lichens lick the lintel with pale determination
in this salt air. These grey walls no longer shelter, or even threaten,
but they frame the black trees, the frail purples
in the snow, the apples, the moon.

Once, long ago, I wrote you a short letter, praising your vision,
seeking recognition from an elder still young. I think you
tried to give that, but it came with a blast of ice
I still feel after many years, words that hardened, did not melt,
my fears, that burned when I turned my mind

to you. Maimed by your brilliance, I was like a pear tree
sliced by lightening. Long after, I spoke to your student.
She said she dreamed of you coming to her room,
cutting her up, stuffing her into a bag. She said
she could only write at night, under covers, with a flashlight.

It has taken me long seasons, struck as I was to the root,
to bloom again. Now I see you offered
what you had to give, an honesty shimmering
with your own pain, an intensity born
in the quest for clarity. Though you met my outstretched hands

with the bite of an axe-blade, you never knew
I stumbled bloody, dazed in wilderness.
Now, I have licked my wounds. No longer a maiden,
I find, little by little, I have remade this landscape. Spring
flows in my veins, I have grown new hands. I praise again. I sing.

# V. Silver Arson

# Orpheus

*for Julia*

It is past the time when the plump rye waves
on its green stalks and apples shine from leaves.

Now the harvest moon is caught on black boughs,
as on the stag's antlers. Breath is frosty.

The time of elegy is come to set
silver arson in the leaf mold under oaks.

Houses lie like lit acorns in the fields,
but to hear the music of the season

you must step into the trees and continue
without light into the big wilderness

where all around you the stripped branches
make a lyre plucked by the chill north wind.

You will want to lie down, but you must
keep moving, finding a way all your own,

guided by the rhythm of your breath
into the circle of cool grey stone.

# Sleeping Beauty in Potter's Field

*for Joy Scantlebury*

I.

Pain is the dark gate,
the keyhole,
the needle's eye.

Beyond lies a vast realm of light,
aurora of ice, a surety
that we are free to intend

if not always to do; to remember
that the briar-bound princess must sleep
before she wakes, must wake when she is kissed;

to know that our best dreams are bedrock
no dawning can shake; that sleep is the potter's wheel
shaping our dreams into spokes of light.

II.

Past this sickle
and the blue sheen of an untimely moon
the northern lights quiver.
Again, that field is new mown.
Soon it will snow.

Snow is hushed
like the wings of angels,
just as stern and comforting.
Snow is the silent refrain
binding the song yearly back on itself.

Ribbons of light
tremble above us like green water,
and here is that blue moon again, the rock
on which we break ourselves
over and over, if we are lucky,

finding inside the blue pearl
of joy, indelible
Joy.

# Jazz

Barn wood weathers—
splinters to silver—
while I wait here
still hoping
those jagged stars
will sing me
to sleep.

# A Candle for Maggie Lee

Lilac. Twilight. Hosta bloom.
Wisteria and tiny dog-tooth violets.
A plum, dewy and unbitten.
Chunks of glittering amethyst,
dark as Elizabeth Taylor's eyes
and cool as a cat's wink, Tulips
almost as black as the skin of an eggplant.
Also, the black light in the Hall of Gems
revealing efflorescence, and that minute bruise
I received who-knows-where. The race-car
sheen of my closed laptop computer.
The crescents of lavender under my daughter's
sleepy eyes . . .

All these extravagant iolite existences now carry
the tinge of you, Maggie Lee, who loved these hues.
They hold your memory in their shadows. Your life
touches mine as I walk beside the flowing Cannon River
or pause on stairs imagined by you,

here in my town,
your town, our town,
where there is, it seems, a constant well
of beauty, purpling and ethereal, renewed and renewing
as the hot petunias in the civic baskets will
do, as drifts of phlox in the Carleton Arb
and that sunset band of cloud on the St. Olaf hill.

## December Rain

Ribbons of water,
chips of confetti,
streetlights aswirl,

traffic lights winking—
red, yellow, green—
and at the tracks, a halting red blinking

and that low, urgent moan
like whale song
breaking in the deep, wet night—

sound gliding on iron rails
into the cold ocean
of stars, of almost snow.

# The Book of Quilts

*Every parting is a death; to join is holy.*


## I. The Photograph
*Hattie Wooddell at 20, Jaspar, Texas*

Wrapped in double wedding rings,
she rocks on the front porch, piecing.
Across from her, a tin love seat.
Above, the shingles, dancing octagons,
carry rain from the roof down
a glittering drain spout back
to the kitchen garden.
Her lap fills with diamonds
colored like new lettuce.


## II. The Pattern

This background
a reverse field:
now crosses,
now stars.
Both dark and the positive, light,
tell of the first split,
birds in flight,
falling,
on sections of blue ether,
pennants of gold like standards,
quadrangles of blood.

III. Prairie Women
*Is it the Lone Star or the Star of Bethlehem?*

They pieced for sanity,
for silence in the wind's continuing,
stasis in the shifting dust.
Their faded dresses,
rose, indigo, black,
warmed the cooling bodies of their dead:
an embrace to last.
They knew, they must have known,
that a central, vivid red, like fire at midnight,
outlives any dark;
that something resides in the groans
of windmills and tight joists,
in shingles creaking, and chicken wire,
and in the long boards of a house,
that some order abides
in even the craziest patched quilt.

# Anniversary

*for Timothy*

In the slow ambling race toward summer's end
we both take last, finishing hand in hand.
The pink poppies lining the way are faded,
replaced by orange-yellow rudbeckia
school-bus bright, tipped with coffee, stiff as frost.

Much becomes clearer as the grass dies,
lies flat against the land. That botanical
coverlet of warm, brown August linen
contrasts with the still-green leaves, as later,
resurrected green lawns will be foils
for fiery maples, sumacs, polished oaks.

As we drift into our fifties, a little
rounder, drier than before, we notice
harvest everywhere: accomplished dreams,
plumping IRAs, more good furniture,
less clutter, fewer longings and regrets.

Now our daughter's laughter floats from the tent
in the back garden, twined with her friend's chirp.
They will fall asleep to whispered secrets,
rise with the new day. Dusk comes. Late fireflies
wink on like the girls' flashlights: semaphores
of continuity and peace, speaking
to watchful parents of possible faith
in seasons to come, journeys not yet launched.

# Memento Mori

How easily certain simple truths
slip from my mind—
for instance, that glass is liquid
and will descend, slower than a glacier,
to thicken the bottom of a window;
that the continents themselves
are drifting, sliding over
a fiery pulp of magma,
and when they collide, so slowly,
they sculpt those mountains
that gather clouds about their peaks
like spun sugar.

Distracted by errant reading glasses,
national politics, the unfolding
beauty of my child, I forget
for weeks at a time
that my own days are numbered,
that the very sun
consumes itself simply by
living its stellar life.

# VI. Cartography of Grief

# Poet Singing

*for Sally Nacker*

There is a broken bird inside her heart.
Her land is winter, full of quiet woe.
The only thing that soothes her is her art.

She feels stunned, like a wounded hind or hart,
a red deer trailing blood across the snow.
There is a broken bird inside her heart.

As wounded things must do, she draws apart,
and grief emerges as her status quo.
The only thing that soothes her is her art.

She must create the spring, so she must start
to conjure, after rain, a fragile bow.
There is a broken bird inside her heart.

She listens, and her memories impart
undying love. She finds a vireo.
The only thing that soothes her is her art.

Her words become a map, a kind of chart;
and, though she sees the way that she will go,
there's still a broken bird inside her heart.
The thing that truly soothes her is her art.

# Cartography of Grief

If the map is flat
must the world be also?
The dining room chairs are askew.

I push them beneath the table,
return to the kitchen;
pour a little wine.

A cello sonata
accompanies
as I mince onions.

Then tears start,
fall—a summer storm,
a little essential seasoning.

Before the doorbell rings,
I remember
to light one yellow candle:

flickering ship's lantern & star to steer by
through all measure of fog,
all the black hours ahead.

# Certain Afternoons

I can actually hear the desuetude
of dusty cups, of rags drying under
the sink—slightly sour—and that brown shape growing,
like a continent, on the white surface
from the tap...tap...tap of city water.

Sometimes I try to imagine my house,
this place, my shell, when I have gone away.
Later, I know these things I hold onto—
so tightly—will scatter—like sparks, like smoke—
to those I love and those I'll never meet.

Someone else will polish my thin pine boards
and watch blue clouds tumble past these sashes.
But first, there will be wider silence;
when dust, a stark presence most able,
will thunder down upon my dry table.

# Our Mutual Undoing

When life can be so uncomfortable
on an ordinary day,
what must death be?

An intensification?
Twisting the bone of discontent
until it snaps?

A tunnel compressing the pain
of a whole life into
a small bolus, dense as plutonium?

Something else? The whack
against a piñata destroys
the fragile form of the body

but, simultaneously,
releases sweet residuals: insights,
dreams, spirit, the seeds (perhaps) of new life.

# What She Wanted Me to Know

*for Lillian Malmquist*

*My husband kissed me and thanked me*
*for every meal I ever made. He treated me*
*like a queen. Roy was Dutch, a wooden shoe.*
*He was too good to live. When he died,*
*after only twenty-six years of marriage, I felt*
*like driving right over the Wabasha Bridge,*
*plunging headfirst into the frozen Mississippi.*

The old woman next door wore a powerful hearing aid,
attached to a microphone. Often the batteries were dead.
She listened to the Twins baseball games in her bathroom;
we could hear the scores next door. It was easiest for her
to hear over the telephone, crackling with amplification.
She called often.

*Flowers ease the mind, calm the nerves. Nothing*
*is so bad that it can't be helped by putting your hands*
*in the dirt. I drove my own car until I was eighty-five.*
*Now, my eyes are too bad. I hire a boy for the yard.*
*The ground is uneven and I am afraid of falling,*
*but just look at my African violets!*

Blind as a bat, she drew witches on gourds and pumpkins
to give us a Halloween treat. She loved to cook, knowing
her recipes by heart, the location of each ingredient, each cup
and spoon, not seeing the grime caked on her refrigerator seals,
beneath her long nails. She served me grilled cheese, perfectly
toasted, delicious when I averted my eyes.

*You really don't eat meat? Not even salmon?*
*I don't understand*

*why people are always on diets. Me, I'm fat as a sausage.*
*I used to cook at the high school. I loved that job, better*
*than the dry cleaners. I think it is wrong,*
*so many women now taking jobs from men.*
*How will the men support their families?*
*Women should stay home.*

Born in 1902, married at forty-two, an only child and childless,
Lil kept her phone number listed under her husband's name
and rarely left the house. The minister came to call.
Her younger cousins—Sister Clara, the retired nun,
Roy who'd devoted himself to his mother
before she passed, Ruth who remarried at seventy-eight
then divorced the next year—they did Lil's marketing,
helped her write her checks, phoned each day.

*This is my mother, in the oval frame. She sold Avon.*
*She had lovely skin. She got confused at the end,*
*but I was able to care for her in her own home.*
*That's how it should be with a daughter.*
*These were her teacups. I want to be here for my birthday.*
*After that, I don't care.*

After we moved away, I came to visit,
brought peach-colored roses to celebrate her ninety years,
drove her around the Minneapolis lakes,
to my house for sherry wine and seafood. The last time
I saw her was at her stucco cottage in West Saint Paul.
I knocked and knocked. Both doors were locked.
It was shocking to see her look out
and wave, smile, refuse, with a little laugh, to open the door.
Her wigs had been obvious, lustrous blonde nylons, Eva Gabors.
I had thought underneath she must be bald, but there she stood,

bent at the waist like a peasant crone, two snowy braids
pinned over her ears. Soon after, a cousin called. They feared
her mind was roaming or gone. They were afraid she'd fall.

*I want a closed casket. I don't want people looking at me*
*when I'm dead. I have put it in writing and the minister knows.*
*Once I went to a medium. Her voice changed, high, like this:*
*"Brown Bear? Brown Bear? Are you there?"*
*Kind of floaty and far away. He was her Indian guide.*
*That was before the war. What do you think*
*happens after you die?  No one will let me talk about my death.*
*They laugh and say I'll live forever.*
*I ask you: Who would want that?*

I visited her twice in the nursing home, a clean, bright place.
She didn't know me. I massaged her shoulders and hushed her
as she cried, pleading with me to take her back home.
When she slipped
into a coma, they called me. I sat by her bedside, weeping,
startling her kin, holding her thin hand, listening
to the rattling gasp of each breath.

*Can't I go now?  I just want to go home.*
*Won't you take me home?*

On the morning she died, a rare white egret
flew past my kitchen window.
Later, I looked down on closed eyelids, her best wig.
The cousins had overruled. A photograph I had taken—
Lillian with her arms filled with my roses—
stood near the casket. I helped
to lift the coffin into the hearse,

then helped to lay it to rest among the acres of white crosses
above the Mississippi, her husband's veteran's plot.
I thought
*Someday I will go back, find her name in that sea of*
*white and green.* But I never have.
Her words are part of me now. When I plunge
my hands into the warm spring soil, when I see the flash
of an egret's wing, I know
Lillian is safe at home;
that she never left, despite the deafening dark.
That none of us is ever lost.
That each breath
can call us home.

# The Apostles

*Bayfield, Wisconsin*

They hold for me the hope of grace
fast in the shape of white sails,
In the rounded, green humps of islands
And the lonesome spruce tree's gothic lift,
in the slender leaning of paper birch.
I watch them all from the shallow harbor,

from safety's most vivid illusion, the harbor,
that ancient metaphor for discovered grace,
saints gliding on frail canoes of birch,
or coracles, or lowering home sails
when the wind dies at sunset. I feel my heart lift
just looking at these few visible islands,

knowing there are more green islands
than the eye can hold. Here, from the harbor,
I can see no break in them. They lift
their backs along the horizon in a graceful,
curved line, appearing like one opposite shore, but sails
slip between them now and then. A veil of birch

snakes down the hillside. The powdery birch
whitens my hands like shed skin. I feel like an island,
I think, my thoughts gliding near like quiet sails,
the truest of them finding some deep harbor
welcoming them home. So this is grace,
I think—to breathe, to lift

my hands sunward and feel my spirits lift
like fog rising to reveal the solid birch.
I almost whisper a plain, remembered grace,
but keep still, silent, like the islands.

I have so much to learn, here in this harbor.
I must learn to work my own sails,

to venture out with only a sound hull, with sails
on a central mast seeking the wind's precarious lift.
On the broken but glittering surface of this harbor,
now that the wind is up, reflections of the birch
are jumbled easily with those of green islands.
I breathe freely, sighing for all this grace.

A harbor is only the starting place. These islands,
Seen through a fog of birch, are stepping stones. They lift
our feet like sails, conferring a resounding grace.

# Black Swans

You can't prove a negative,
but sometimes it turns up
true, despite
experience and reasonable doubt.

No one in England
had ever seen a black swan;
ergo, no one had looked
upside down, in Australian lagoons.

The capacity for faith
might be a blind urge
to squeeze meaning from the dry
rock of random chance;

or faith might be the knack
of seeing those luminous fields
surrounding hard facts, those currents we
move in, like magnetized flecks of iron.

Faith is as sturdy
and necessary as a rope bridge—
a slender, swaying path,
holding just one foot at a time.

Behind, white swans sun themselves on familiar rocks;
ahead, black swans gather in unimaginable flocks.

# Musings at the New River Bridge

*New River Gorge, West Virginia*

Sooner or later, we must all cross it.
In a moment or two, we all must go
so high we brush the sun-touched clouds,
appear glorious, strange, changed before we vanish
on the other side.

This mysterious New River cuts us
gorgeously from what we know. Will we
greet old friends on the other bank? Do
they wait to embrace us? We know only
legend. Vision. Many fears. Hope.

And tears. Though why should truth be cloaked
by hymnal dusts? I see diamonds dancing
in raging mist. This always-New River is
primeval, irrefutable. I hope
that on the day when I take

my high climb I shall remember to pause
at the top of the arc and look back—
seeing, finally, before I drop
from your sight, all the wonder
of my life—those lovely ripples I made.

# The Extinction of Myths

Even mythological creatures, the immortal ones,
can go extinct. Yet, they can also be revived,
those old stories of yearning and wonder
and terror. All it takes is a pen or brush,
a few hushed words by the fireside, a child
or old man gazing at the stars:

Look! the glowing tail of Pegasus,
bright as a comet; all those incandescences—
golden leaves like flames, feathers of the phoenix
burning, a bird content in its suffering. And the silver
scimitar of that moonlit river, washing us all
back to the primordial, opalescent pulse of the heavens.

# Rain Clouds to the East

The dawning light bounces, rosy and buoyant,
to the center of the sky, while off to the east
grey reigns, dragging its iron scepter—
ragged clouds, low and scudding—
over the auroran edge of the world.

Nearer, trees rise up like lollipops—
lime, white, pink, and red—buds tight
and dense as raindrops. At the street corner,
a stop sign stands like a cartoon tulip:
a sentry guarding the crossing
of one inscrutable season into another.

Meanwhile, as rain ticks against the windows,
lilacs distill their periwinkle memorial fragrance.
Somewhere, cradled by twig, a blue-green egg waits.

# Notes

Elegies are love songs for our dead, the people and possibilities now lost though still very real and resonant in our hearts. To take true joy in the beauty of life requires a parallel ability to abide with the obsidian fact of death and grey mist of grief. My temperament and circumstances in childhood sensitized me to loss on a variety of levels, but it was when I was a senior in college that I discovered the necessity of elegy. My induction into this tradition jolted me in such a way that I was changed forever.

On March 4, 1981, the day after my brother's eighteenth birthday, I learned that he had been in a fatal accident. Asked to read at his memorial service, I was led to a magnificent cathedral of a poem (495 lines in 55 Spenserian stanzas), written by Percy Bysshe Shelley for his friend, John Keats, whose death in 1821 at age twenty-five was an untimely tragedy for us all. Shelley's elegy for his friend offers the tripartite movement of classic elegy: general lament for our own mortality, praise for the departed loved one, and a measure of consolation. I excerpted a tiny percentage of the whole poem to share at Kurt's memorial service. These lines are near the conclusion: "Life, like a dome of many-colored glass / Stains the white radiance of Eternity..." and they have consoled me since I first spoke them before a host of mourners. My own first elegies, sparked by my brother's death, showed me the power of this essential genre, and have led to this collection.

"Encountering Catacombs" The Catacombs of Paris are still open; the site is now one of fourteen city museums managed by Paris Musées. I visited when I was fifteen and in Paris without my family. One enters under a scripted warning: "Arrête! C'est ici l'empire de la Morte." Back then, one traveled through the dark tunnels without the benefit of electricity, the way lighted only by carrying a lit candle. Recently locating the entrance on a map, I was interested to see that this subterranean gateway is only a few blocks from the Paris Observatory with its celestial orientation.

"My Father Confessor" This poem celebrates the influence on my life of one key teacher, Leo Luke Marcello, whom I met during my graduate studies in Lake Charles. When he visited me ten years later, he told me about his poems celebrating the life of Katherine Drexel (1858-1955); seven years after our visit, she became the second canonized saint of the Roman Catholic Church to have been born an American citizen. Leo and I also spent time at the Minneapolis Institute of Art together and were able to see in process the east-west, high tech-low tech, spiritual-scientific collaboration between Tibetan Buddhist monks and 3M scientists. The resulting mandala now hangs in the gallery of Asian art, where visitors can also find the Chinese watchtower model that sparked another poem. The Minneapolis Museum of Art is a peerless resource for my life as an artist.

"Homesick" was inspired by my reading of Lucy Newlyn's insightful literary biography *William and Dorothy Wordsworth: All in Each Other* (Oxford University Press, 2013); this work also influenced my poem "On Biography". I had in mind, especially, the Wordsworth home known as Rydal Mount in England's Lake District.

"Mortua Est" (June 2015), "Still Life with Poppies" (July 2015), and "The Scattering" (August 2015) This trio of poems was written in response to my grief at the sudden death of my aunt, Shirley Marie Pressel Warden; they also express my joy in the ways her life intersects with my own.

"Triptych" Like the poems for my brother, this one is for a young person who died too soon. Jennifer Bonner—a daughter of my neighbors, a gifted visual artist, and a Carleton College student—was someone who taught me indelible lessons of humor, wisdom, and graceful kindness under the mortal pressure we all face.

"Plumbago" This section is the anatomy of a brief first marriage that began in Wisconsin and finally foundered in Louisiana, just a year before my former husband took his life at Christmas time. The title poem, "Plumbago," refers to the subtropical flowering shrub, also known as leadwort, with blue blossoms; the name of the plant is derived from the Latin word for that soft, toxic metal.

"Eclipse at Solstice" Seven years prior to committing suicide, my father announced his intentions to end his life one day to avoid the indignities he saw as the inevitable endgame for someone who had Parkinson's disease. Seven years after he exercised this option early in December, I found the dark of the holiday period particularly hard to bear. To cope, I began writing sonnets to understand my constellation of emotions. It was the visit of a friend which helped light my way out of this sadness. After her visit, I wrote the fifth and final sonnet of the series, all of which were composed within a twenty-four-hour period.

"Sleeping Beauty in Potter's Field" This poem celebrates the life of poet Joy Scantlebury, a classmate of mine at McNeese State University's M.F.A. program. Joy was the person who introduced me to the work of Amy Clampitt. It was through Joy's efforts that Clampitt visited McNeese and I was then able to meet her, receive her critiques, and begin a long correspondence with that master poet. Composed in response to Leo Luke Marcello's invitation to contribute a poem to a festschrift for Joy, my poem (a Clampitt-esque lyric) seeks to honor her sense of wonder, her curiosity in the face of death from lung cancer, and her zest for language.

"A Candle for Maggie Lee" Sometimes one briefly and superficially intersects with a legendary person and is forever changed by the encounter. Maggie Lee spent ten minutes once interviewing me for one of her columns in the *Northfield News*, and I learned that this vigorous and lively purple-clad elder had, prior to retirement, been the longtime editor of the paper and the driving force behind the development of Northfield's beautiful riverfront. Maggie Lee continues to inspire me with her evident love of her craft and her hometown. For me, she is an exemplar of how one person can make a real and positive difference for everyone just by working hard at what he or she loves.

"The Book of Quilts" While working on an M.F.A. degree and teaching freshman composition, I desperately needed a non-verbal escape. It was then I leaped from simply admiring and reading about quilts to making them. This poem encapsulates many streams of thought about the relationships of art-making in all forms to life as it is lived. It was inspired by a classic text, *The Quilters*, by Patricia Cooper and Norma Bradley Allen. This book juxtaposes oral history of pioneer quilt makers in the American southwest at the turn of the twentieth century with photographs of these artists, their quilts, and the objects in daily life (log cabins, field rows) that gave rise to quilt patterns they used. I was especially intrigued by their knowledge of how different colors of dyed fabrics fade at different rates.

"Musings at the New River Bridge" The bridge that spans the New River in West Virginia rivals the Eiffel Tower for elegance and function. The New River gorge is spectacular and dramatic, in some places plunging 1,000 feet down to the river that carved it; the New River is thought to be the oldest river system in the world.

## About the Author

Leslie Schultz can't remember a time when she wasn't making poems. She studied creative writing at the UW-Madison in Madison, WI and at McNeese State University in Lake Charles, LA. She now lives in Northfield, Minnesota. Born contemplative and prone to leaps of faith, she began studying yoga as a teenager and has never stopped. In the 1990s, she fell in love with labyrinths, built one in her own garden, and walked it daily. In 1998, Schultz completed yoga teacher training at Kripalu Center in Lenox, MA and co-founded Heartwork Yoga Studio. In 2000, she began collaborating with artist and labyrinth maker Marilyn Larson to publish contemplative resources, including *A Pocket Guide to Labyrinths*; four printings later, it is still available at Grace Cathedral in San Francisco. Schultz's photography has been purchased by hospitals, clinics, and private collections, and is featured on greeting cards. Her poetry, fiction, and essays have appeared a variety of journals and anthologies, including *Able Muse*; *Mezzo Cammin*; *Swamp Lily*; *Poetic Strokes Anthology*; *The Pacific Review*; *The Northern Review*; *The Madison Review*; *The Mid-American Poetry Review*; *The Midwest Quarterly; Stone Country*; *Sun Dog*; *The Wayfarer*; and in a chapbook, *Living Room* (Midwestern Writers' Publishing House). In 2013, one of her haiku was included in the payload of NASA's MAVEN mission and is currently orbiting the red planet. She has published two middle-grade novels, featuring main characters who are homeschooled, with Do Life Right Press: *The Howling Vowels* (2011) and *And Sometimes Y* (2013). Schultz posts poems, essays, interviews, and photographs at *www.winonamedia.net*.

Made in the USA
Middletown, DE
14 August 2016